SHE

ALSO BY M.L. ROSENTHAL

POETRY

Blue Boy on Skates, Oxford University Press, 1964
Beyond Power, Oxford University Press, 1969
The View from the Peacock's Tail, Oxford University Press, 1972

CRITICISM

The Modern Poets: A Critical Introduction, Oxford University
    Press, 1960
The New Poets: American and British Poetry since World War II,
    Oxford University Press, 1967
Poetry and the Common Life, Oxford University Press, 1974

SHE

poems
by

M.L. ROSENTHAL

Cover Illustration by
Richard Pousette-Dart

BOA EDITIONS • BROCKPORT, N.Y. • 1977

Grateful acknowledgment is made to the following publications in which some of these poems first appeared: *American Poets in 1976* (The Bobbs-Merrill Co.): "We Begin These Things Lightly," "Riddle of The Swan," "Suddenly at the Edge," "Bequest"; *The American Poetry Review:* "Fable of The Mermaid and The Drunks" (Pablo Neruda); *The Humanist:* "Intimacy"; *Modern Poetry Studies:* "Through Streets Where Smiling Children"; *The Nation:* "Compleynte, etc.," "The Darkest Dream"; *New Review* (London): "Riddle of The Swan," "Imagining You Leaving Tangier Before a Storm," "Variation on a Theme by Rilke," "Bequest"; *The New Yorker:* "From a Distance"; *New York Quarterly:* "Joy"; *Ontario Review:* "We Begin These Things Lightly"; *Parnassus:* "She"; *Present Tense:* "Albatross," "Night Vision (1973); *Salmagundi:* "First Time-Song," "Second Time Song," "Variation on a Theme by Rilke."

The author and the publisher also wish to thank the Andrew Crispo Gallery for permission to reproduce the work of Richard Pousette-Dart.

Designed and printed at the Visual Studies Workshop, Rochester, New York.
Typeset by Advertising and Marketing Graphics.
Binding by Gene Eckert, Inc.

ISBN 0-918526-05-1 Cloth
   0-918526-06-X Paper

First Edition: December, 1977

In times to come,
it may be,
it will please us
to remember these things.

∽ ORDER OF THE SEQUENCE ∾

Tonight the stars are close.
They glitter so fiercely down
everything she says and is
points the long arrow toward my heart.
I'll lay me down
on early April's sparse, cold grass
and stare up through the cirrus clouds
into her clear heaven-wells
each with its naked glittering star.
It is the naked constellation, She,
and bends her glittering bow,
each arrow true to its mark.

SHE

She writes of sunburnt thighs,
a terrace of stone lions,
and Naxos just visible from her window.

This poor vessel, I,
one-oared, rudderless, droops
or, randy, unspent, shivers
in the moist night
towards gardens blowing where she sleeps or wakes. Dawn
is breaking there. And at its eastern gate
erratic trumpets blast their notes of war.
I'll beat into the wind as best I can.

Tack and turn as we will
close to or before the wind
whatever beats in the blood
can never be forgone.

I have been imagining
a small girl staring
through flawed crystal
at bombed babies, keening mothers.

Where gulls swoop for offal flung from freighters
and Oceanides flash their pearls of spray,
the thought of losing you washes over me again,
then sweeps back, away into the great sea.

There's
where the hawk must hang, sea-garden grow, battered pinnace
ride the abyss, sinking and rising, so.

RIDDLE OF THE SWAN

Once, beating through the air, you amazed us.
We smiled under your shadow.

Broken-winged and raucous now, you're borne
whithersoever the torrent lists.

She and I, flung high on that arc where you made your song,
    never before saw
our joined shadows beating and riding the torrent below.

WE BEGIN THESE THINGS LIGHTLY

We begin these affairs lightly
with an obscure smile, or an unseeing glance.

The soul, flung like rags on a greasy floor,
wavers into oneness again, tiny flames flickering.

ECSTASY

No more, then, to wander talking
into the querulous, misty, intimate hills?
Have you strayed too far from the others?
Do you shy away now, angry and anxious?

Still, after all, it's here —
a forgetting, not a death.
A hand touches, a banner flutters.
Over us, now, something waits and watches.

FROM A DISTANCE

    Miles off
you have your separate day.
Perhaps you lightly carry
my yesterday's body, memory's mannequin,
within yourself as I
drift in yours — cohabitants
of one another's quickened space.

It's here, though, everything unravels
in broad daylight, no place to go.
Gossamer tightropes dwindling to pollen.
Heart pounding as day and night converge.

Mule-kick of heart and brain, getting too excited.
I've got to get myself under control.
Something like a clear chime just to hold steady,
clean winter lines, a bright day just like this,
nothing disastrous, just remote, cool as your warm, absent kiss.

IMAGINING YOU LEAVING TANGIER
BEFORE A STORM

A wind blowing in Tangier. And you leaving, "heavy
    with luggage."
Hard to dismiss you from the mind's retina and let
    you be
one hustled mite in the mob scattered by the whimsy
of a Moroccan wind all but into the harbor. The
    dock-loungers
stare "Tourist-with-Frightened-Eyes" at you. You're
    blown scurrying
onto the ship. And the old passengers, coming off, are hit
by the gusty darkness that lifts you so passionately
to ride on the swart seething seas. O, brave exchange!

I'm swept off the ship into black Tangier. The rain
finds me naked in its soaking chill. Coughing, my wallet
    already stolen,
I'm stripped by mumbling beggars, booked by the port
    police,
and hanged at dawn. And you, have you reached Algeciras
    yet?

FIRST TIME-SONG

If I am very still, I may not be able to tell
how painfully the earth, shriek though it may
    through space,
turns. and turns. and turns. and turns. and creaks
on its rusted axletree. and creaks. until it stops
entirely. God! let me off
until the thing's cranked up again, and time
begins, again, to slip away so fast
it blisters everything that clings to it.

SECOND TIME-SONG

The hours inch by, the days yield not at all.
The steady weeks hold stoutly at their posts.

All day the honking cars and hooting boats
stream their hard designs of north and south.

Can I dream myself into oblivion?
If I rest my forehead on this hard old desk?

The clocks may race, the calendar's on strike.
Who shall roll this heavy time up and over the hill?

COMPLEYNTE, ETC

I cannot wait another day, and another day, yet do.
The waste of golden time clings to my fingers.
We're so ringed round with absence I can hardly move
toward you without a sudden leap of prayer.

Yet that famous golden laughter of the gods
invades me, amid these slipping days and nights,
these maelstroms, balked dreams, balancings
on snarling walls. Oh, two cosmic, comic acrobats

have swung from the bright hooked tips of the crescent moon
clasping, unclasping among the bristling hours
with a *ha-ha-ha* and a *hey, nonny-no*
and cries of *Impetuous Pistil!* and *Ah! sweet Stamen!*

INTIMACY

With flagrant fingers
I fling wide the window
upon our opened world.

How intimate our world
with all the loving
man-and-woman smells.

Did you think I didn't love
the smell of you?
Idiot!

Not that the four blackbirds
screeching and scooting past
are intimate with us, not that they give a damn.

Ah but this opened world
is intimate with them
whether they give a damn or not.

BY MY TROTH

I want
    nothing dearer
    than what I await
    with believing, unbelieving heart
    day by day.

I think
    of you moving
    in rooms far from me.
    The telephone! the postman!
    I'll shower them with kisses.

I know
    we are not one.
    Other lives and loves
    in rooms far from me
    have possessed you.

I have
    found you —
    death to the contrary.
    If our souls are ships
    adrift on the same sea,
    I want nothing dearer.

FABLE OF THE MERMAID AND THE DRUNKS

All these guys were inside there
when she came in the door completely naked
they were drunk they started spitting at her
she didn't understand she'd just come up out of the river
she was only a mermaid who'd lost her way
their insults splattered her bright flesh
their obscenities smeared her breasts of gold
she didn't know about crying she didn't cry
she didn't know about dressing she had no clothes on
they stubbed out their cigarettes on her and marked her
    up with burnt cork
they laughed so hard they were rolling on the tavern floor
she didn't say anything she didn't know about talking
her eyes were the color of far-off love
her arms were made of matching topazes
her lips moved silently in a coral light
at last she left by that same door
she'd hardly plunged back in the river when she was clean
    again
shining like a white stone in the rain again
and without looking back she swam off once more
swam off to the void swam off to die

from the Spanish of Pablo Neruda

LONG NIGHT

Between the dark and the daylight
longing that mutes itself to the tick of the drifting minutes
these weary dreams on the seas of others' sleep
one-tick-and-then-another and the eyes neither closed nor
    open
Who so list to hount I know beyond the Alps
where is an hynde lies Italy   She opes to the searching
    touch
of these drifting fingers of dream her warm turning
sole self bright with her white marvels her eyes
of night her remembering thoughts her waking
portals of delight   And the long night narrows
to an hour's sleep just after dawn.

I KNOW WHERE IS AN HYNDE

The doe and her three fawns have returned.
They've crossed the hurtling highway from the mountain
just for crab apples, or our delight.
If we approach they freeze, and then
westward into one wood flies the doe,
eastward, into the other, the three fawns go.

Strange how some acid of the mind
burns away the bruise of days
yet leaves this glow of our delight.
And we here now, talking and caressing,
know love holds steady, that began before we knew,
though fawn must run at last where doe cannot pursue.

These autumn woods blaze up for our delight.
These leaves are fire
that love kindled, in forgotten other seasons.
Follow the doe's trail back up the mountain
to our own voices glowing in the mist — both she
and we flame there, fed by all memory.

Over and over I've thought never to forget
even the tiniest broken creature by the highway,
yet hardly remember souls I've clambered after
fanatical, will-o'-the-wisps on the trail of our delight.
The doe and her fawns feed under the crab apple tree.
Dear love, we know how sweet their breaths must be.

INCANTATION

First, to say your name aloud. Then, touch your cheek.
Then, stretch my whole length of self against
the warm length of you and hold you, thus, until
yet once more, again, the loaves and fishes multiply.

I say your name aloud. I touch your cheek.
I stretch my whole length of self against
the warm length of you and hold you, thus, until,
yet once more, again, the loaves and fishes multiply.

Slash of sea-wind. Stab of wild-rose thorn.
Violent heaped sunlight of our days.
Harshness of your love-gasp. Glittering circlet of your name.

ONCE

"Mistress," I said to her
whose name is body of my desire,
"will these green days
remain with us forever?"

"Mistress," I said to her
whose name is all my thought,
"I had forgot
the very name of Death.
Desire for Her blew through me once like the mistral."

A cold, forgotten voice replied,
"Desire blew through us once like the mistral."

VARIATION ON A THEME BY RILKE
("Einmal, wenn ich dich verlier")

Some day, when I lose you,
clear as, real as, today,
will we think, *This is the very day,*
golden and blue, that's the last day?

When space and time, for once, hold firm,
never to return upon themselves,
will we two, touching and listening,
think to think, *This day leaves no shadow?*

Will we feel only the usual desolation
settling on us until . . . the next time?
Or will we think, *But this day stands alone?*
This is the day that, for once, has no end?

BEQUEST

Burn our sweet story,
let the wind carry its smoke away.
Hasten, hasten —
leave no shred to betray
our names, where we went, why we lingered,
whom we loved, when we wept, on what day.

ALBATROSS

Near the Wailing Wall

an old woman in the sun

        head hanging

NOT QUITE METAPHYSICAL

Is this the real you, then?
Or is it the real you of my imagination, then?
And shall I trouble myself about which is which?

A man doesn't want to be a fool,
at least not the kind of fool
he doesn't want to be

in the ironical eye
of a sensible woman
who keeps her own sensible counsel.

THE DARKEST DREAM

I used this word, "joy,"
as my argument.
But misery lacks words —
there's no debate.

I used it, next,
as my talisman.
But misery is blind —
there's no remission.

And then, suddenly,
I could no longer say
it even to you —
so mute is misery.

SUDDENLY AT THE EDGE

Suddenly at the edge, black ocean below,
and over the edge, flight without wings,
soughing of waves, stillness of star-pierced air,
tight-clenched and silent motion.

                            Soughing of leaves
now in my memory
holds, like your smile flickering towards me,
buoyant tracers ablaze, as when you
woke lovely and drowsy and lay down beside me
and we played like dolphins, awash in the night.

NIGHT VISION (1973)

What is this bitter taste — your long absence.
Glistening berries sicken on the vine.

Candle-dim, across light-years,
your white shoulder rising above my head,

and, above the stilled kingdoms of glittering days,
the trees of night looming from forgotten graves.

Cold flash of light among the unmoving shades:
fireflies flicker against the tree-trunks.

Crack of a bullet in the silent street
and the skull, shattered, too heavy with history.

Young killers thunder over ancient villages.
Crackling flesh replies to the tongues of flames.

SAINT

Eternal
"You,"
bless me among
Your other phalloi.

If I am gentle
do not think me
less fierce
than You.

So many
crimson with pride
do not know
I am proud too.

This calling dust,
under the sky's
blazing clock:
"I."

JOY

From some cold place in the great wobbling chaos
we have entered each other's forests and skies.

You are there. I see you when I dare to look.
Somewhere, once, was the place
where I knew this arrival must some day be so.

Waves of all force enter us from all that surrounds us.
Our hearts are beating steady as we wander
out of all space into each other's forests and skies.

Now I stand upright within your deepest, greenest glade
here, where we speak of plainest, most needful things.
Around me, above me, your face, your voice, holding steady.

THROUGH STREETS WHERE SMILING CHILDREN

Sometimes, out of your woman world,
your other memories, times, spaces, faces,
the chill of otherness blows across
our grove. You say a truth that's of
yourself, not us. My sloe-eyed darling, nobody's rich
as you. You
want me to speak how we are, and your own clear voice
rises up out of me, the other I
in its other sphere, making things clear,
sorting us out. Lying here, caressed,
caressing your breasts, the swell of your thighs,
marvelous plains of your flanks where armies of kisses march,
roused by the honeydew of your murmuring mouth,
I'll bring charges in no court of law against
your otherness. You are. And I have seen, too,
the chill of steel beams — no, the high oaks,
distant, unto themselves, of your quick thought's slow
     flourishing.

Say your television cops and cries of "Bullshit!"
cut across our dreams like iodine splashes.
Cafés in Paris, the Luxembourg Gardens, hand-to-mouth
     romance
on the run till I expire of ecstasy in some sweaty garret
while you, Eve Curie, go on to glory
wearing my poems between your perfumed breasts —
Bullshit. Begin again, then,
something that will work, a plainer plan. Still,
we improvise it all out of bits and pieces, dream-shards.
Everything you've dreamt has brought me to this grove, and
     you to me.
Everything I've dreamt too.

You have gathered the violence of your heart
into ordered days and places. Sunlight bathes you
in wavering lines, near tiny tropical fish
whose fins shimmer in luminous green amid
the bubbles streaming and bursting about them.
You wear your passion lightly, like a summer frock,
through streets where smiling children kick
each other's heads, twist each other's penises,
past hallways where broken beings retch unheard,
where blood drips from women cowed by unseen fists.
(Perhaps he will finish her off with switchblade and prick,
some slum Don Giovanni, proud killer and lover,
seizing her breasts for his instant of triumph, his accolade
        her paralyzed scream.)
You have gathered the violence of your heart's need
into clear spaces for the soul's ordering: your mind
at the ready, wearing your life lightly,
as the trees outside your window keep thrusting upward,
        "lightly."

You think you are alone. The sunlight comes in through
        your window
and finds you gravely at your desk or, poised among saucers,
manuscript, stove, and phonograph, juggling the long hours
with "so much to do." What is a "vision"? Your face, in
        laughter or repose,
shadow or light. Your self, very still or walking on a street,
or poured like nectar into a voice I drink from all hours.

FOR A MOMENT

— As if, after all, it has gone.
Defined, snapped shut, buried.
                            And all still alive back there,
the shades, the levels of green you loved. Still there.

Even a ghost has things, except to die, to do.

Did you ever imagine, as a child,
these silences falling away
from where death watched us for a moment
and then the mockingbird's manic medley
wild with the morning, wild for heaven to notice.